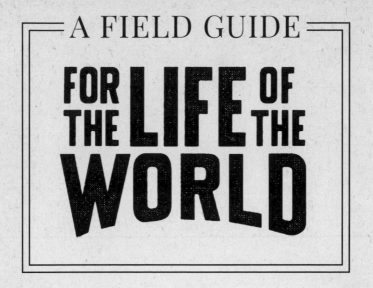

A FIELD GUIDE

FOR THE LIFE OF THE WORLD

A FIELD GUIDE

FOR THE LIFE OF THE WORLD

Letters to the Exiles

Branding design by DOMOREGOOD | csk
Developed, written, and edited by Heidi Segal

Executive Publishers: Brett Elder, Stephen Grabill
Contributors: Evan Koons, Jonathan Witt

WELCOME "NOT HOME"

TRAIL GUIDES: EPISODES 1 - 7

BEFORE WE EMBARK

Everybody,

It might be helpful to explain a few things about this handy field guide—to get our bearings before we head out.

Inside you'll find an **INTRODUCTION** with:

An introduction **Letter** from me: I begin with a little "behind the scenes" explanation for this film series.

A Series Trailer: Enjoy a sneak peak of the entire series before taking the first step on our wonderful journey. You'll find this on the *For the Life of the World: Letters to the Exiles* DVD in the Extras section or accessed at StudySpace.org.

The **Story of Exile**: This is a short dive into the historical meaning and experience of life *not home*.

The Cast: You'll learn a little more about the gift-givers on our journey.

My illustrated **Field Guide Map** trailer: It charts out key destinations on our expedition (available in the *For the Life of the World: Letters to the Exiles* DVD Extras section or in the *Field Guide: For the Life of World* digital version at StudySpace.org).

Field Sightings: These are a few photos I collected that focus on significant objects of interest in the series.

And finally, the **Hall of Scholars**: I created a t-shirt series of inspiring field scholars and fellow explorers.

...

You'll also find seven **TRAIL GUIDES,** one for each episode. Each includes:

Letter from Evan (yes, me): I'll introduce the themes and ideas explored in each episode, and hopefully kick-start your group's creative investigation. We'll take a close survey of what it means to live as the church in exile, on planet Earth.

Episode Teaser: Each episode has its very own video trailer to give you a foreshadowing of our journey. (Check them out on the DVD or at StudySpace.org.)

Friends on the Journey: I'll reveal who will join us for each episode and how each will uncover some particularly amazing discoveries along the way. (You can find more about them in "The Cast" section of the introduction.)

The Landscape: We'll encounter concepts and phrases that help grow our understanding of what it means to be pilgrims and strangers living in the *not yet now*. (Feel free to put them in your pockets for later use.)

Studio Work | *Idea Exchange:* Here we'll have the opportunity to discuss the journey—all that we've seen and heard.

Porch Steps | *Hello World:* And then we can put our discoveries into action. We'll consider ways to live as salt and light in the world, by the Holy Spirit's transformative power. (Relying on our own strength and brain power does not work so well, I've found.)

Lantern Light: Light for our path is essential. So we'll read key Scripture texts to help us understand the theme of exile throughout the Bible. We'll find crucial wisdom for our life journey. Let's go deep, where the marrow is (Heb. 4:12).

Prayer Journal: God calls us to pray without stopping. But why do we pray? If we connect with God throughout our day, it's hard to forget he is with us and for us. We also know prayer changes us. And when God transforms us to mirror his image, the blessed gifts of God overflow in fellowship. Let us pray.

Read More: *For the Life of the World: Letters to the Exiles* is rooted in some seriously profound Biblical field scholarship. In this section, I'll list key materials that inspired each episode. Want to explore further? Check out these resources!

Yours, Evan

WELCOME "NOT HOME"

Dear Everybody,

I'm Evan. I'm just like you.

I live at my place, here in *Peregre Exilium* (Latin for "Exile Abroad," and happens to be the same place you live).

And it has come to my attention that I might not have answers to some basic questions about this redeemed life I am living.

You hear the word *exile*. You're told you're in it. Strangers in a strange land, on your way home.

So what is my place and purpose in this God-created world that surrounds me?

As I walk this earthy ground:

Should I don a helmet and hazmat suit?

Or huff and puff, shouldering a fifty-pound tome on worldly warfare, ready for aim at anything out of line?

Should I casually wear the same clothes as everyone else, sip the same drinks or carry the same reading material, quietly unnoticeable?

Maneuvering all three methods at any given moment could work. The *fortification-domination-accommodation* triple blend. Hmmmm. (You'll learn more about this later.)

I thought I understood where I was going and what I should be doing along the way. Instead, I find myself hiding. Or fighting. Or blending into a world that I forget is not my home.

Is there a plan, an approach, a calling?

Perhaps we need a new, wider lens for understanding what it means to be in the world, not of it.

Thankfully, I know some gift-giving souls who can help.

Sit down on a couch for a moment (or even a chair will do).

Grab a glass of lemonade, which happens to be my favorite thirst quencher.

We will be doing some grand exploring in this series, and that might work up a thirst ... for more.

I'll write again soon.

Yours, Evan

P.S. Maybe this whole thing works like a tiny acorn.

STORY OF EXILE

Who are these exiles receiving letters, and what does it have to do with me?

Hey Everybody,

You know all of those historical accounts about ancient Israel in the Bible? I've been wondering. Just what, exactly, do they have to do with God's plan for us, the church in the world, today? Are we woven into the same historical tapestry? Authors of the New Testament use the word *exile* to describe our present journey in the world. We are "exiles" (1 Pet. 1:1,17), "foreigners and exiles" (1 Pet. 2:11) with a heavenly citizenship (Phil. 3:20; Heb. 13:14) and a hope for the kingdom come. Israelites in the Old Testament also experienced a temporary stay in exile with the hope of a future kingdom restoration. I think there must be a deeper story that connects these exilic journeys.

Throughout the Old Testament, the kingdom of Israel had its share of ups and downs. When Israel yearned after God, she thrived in a blazing-bright culture. When she turned her heart from God, darkness and destruction followed. Solomon's reign was a golden age of wealth and wisdom in Jerusalem. Even the Queen of Sheba paid a visit to check it out for herself. But those glory days came to an end when Israel's kings no longer hungered for a relationship with God, their creator. (Like Adam and Eve, Israel thought autonomy from God would give them power and life, rather than death.) Jeremiah the prophet records how Israel was exiled to Babylon for its faithlessness.

A spiraling event like this would typically signal the end of a story, a tragedy without hope. But take a closer look at Jeremiah 29. God gives Jeremiah a very important and illuminating message for the leaders of Israel. It's a strange message, with a hopeful future. The Israelites are forced to live in a foreign, antagonistic culture, and yet, God commands them to build, plant, and have families, and to "seek the peace and prosperity" (29:7) of their new neighbors. God also promises to restore Israel in Jerusalem after a lifetime in exile. Israel's restoration was rooted in a continuum of fruitful endeavors in a foreign country, the people living in hope that one day they would return home. This work would not only transform their surroundings. The Israelite's labor would transform them as a people of God. This is sounding quite familiar, isn't it?

As the church in the world, we are not home, yet. We are called to good endeavors in the world, wherever we live (Eph. 2:10). We may want to create our own little Jerusalems, waiting out our exile in comfort and security, but Jesus calls us to be salt and light in a world wrestling with decay and darkness. Salt and light permeate and have an impact on whatever they touch. They transform by their very presence. In the same way, we are called to engage our cultural surroundings and have a faithful presence in our communities. I think this means we are called to be present and accessible in every sphere of culture, whether it be work, art, education, government, or our church. It all comes down to being ready to share the hope we have in Christ, and being ready to love with Christ's love by the power of the Holy Spirit—everywhere, every day, every moment, in everything we do (Col. 3:23-24).

You've probably sojourned awhile on this planet Earth and discovered that life in exile is not easy. Living *not home* requires patience, perseverance, and sacrifice, which are not things I naturally keep on hand. Thankfully, we know a source with infinite supply for the entire journey. "And my God will meet all your needs according to the riches of his glory in Christ Jesus" (Phil. 4:19).

Yours, Evan

THE CAST

Here are some gift-givers you'll meet on our journey.

DR. ANTHONY BRADLEY

DR. ANTHONY BRADLEY

Anthony B. Bradley is an author, professor, lecturer, TV commentator, and cultural critic. Recognized as an authority on issues of race, political economy, welfare policy, religion, hip hop, youth culture, and human flourishing, Bradley has appeared on C-SPAN, NPR, CNN/Headline News, and Fox News, among other news outlets. His books include *Black and Tired, Liberating Black Theology*, and *Aliens in the Promised Land*.

Bradley is associate professor of theology and ethics at The King's College in New York City and research fellow at renowned think tank Acton Institute. Previously, Bradley was assistant professor of systematic theology and ethics at Covenant Theological Seminary in St. Louis, where he also directed the Francis A. Schaeffer Institute. His degrees include a B.S. in biological sciences from Clemson University, an M.Div. from Covenant Theological Seminary, an M.A. in ethics and society from Fordham University, and a Ph.D. in philosophy from Westminster Theological Seminary.

DR. AMY SHERMAN

Amy L. Sherman is a senior fellow at the Sagamore Institute for Policy Research, where she directs the Center on Faith in Communities. Sherman also serves as a senior fellow at the International Justice Mission's IJM Institute, a leading Christian human rights agency engaged in the fight against human trafficking. She is the editorial director for FASTEN, a capacity-building project for faith-based organizations, and the founder and former executive director of Charlottesville Abundant Life Ministries, an Evangelical nonprofit assisting low-income, inner-city families. She has served on the advisory board of the Christian Community Development Association for several years.

Dr. Sherman is the author of six books and over seventy-five published articles in periodicals such as *Christianity Today, First Things, The Public Interest, Policy Review, Prism, The Christian Century*, and *Books & Culture*.

Her undergraduate degree is from Messiah College and her graduate degrees are from the University of Virginia. Sherman's life verse is Micah 6:8.

DR. JOHN PERKINS

DR. JOHN PERKINS

John Perkins and his family have been ministering among the poor for the last thirty-nine years. In 1960, Perkins left a "successful" life in California and moved back to Mendenhall, Mississippi, to begin ministry. Founding Mendenhall Ministries, the Perkins family helped start a day-care center, a youth program, a church, an adult education program, a cooperative fair, a thrift store, a housing-repair ministry, and a health center.

Perkins founded Voice of Calvary Ministries, a Christian community development ministry in Jackson, which planted a church, a health center, a leadership development program, a thrift store, a low-income housing development, and a training center.

In northwest Pasadena, Perkins founded Harambee Christian Family Center, ministering to a neighborhood that had one of the highest daytime crime rates in California.

Currently, Perkins serves as the co-founder and chairman of the Christian Community Development Association. The CCDA has over 600 organizational members and 3,000 individual members in over one-hundred cities.

DR. STEPHEN GRABILL

DR. STEPHEN GRABILL

Stephen Grabill is director of programs and senior research scholar in theology at Acton Institute for the Study of Religion and Liberty. He teaches social ethics in an adjunct capacity at Grand Rapids Theological Seminary.

He is the general editor of the *NIV Stewardship Study Bible*; author/editor of eight books in diverse fields such as social ethics, economic history, and theology; founding editor and now editor emeritus of *Journal of Markets & Morality*; general editor (along with Jordan Ballor) of Abraham Kuyper's *Common Grace* translation and the multivolume *Opening the Scriptures* series; and the publisher of Christian's Library Press, Acton Institute's publishing imprint.

He is responsible for providing strategic direction and oversight to Acton's evangelical outreach efforts through network building, content creation, and intellectual innovation. He serves on the Stewardship Council board, as well as the board of advisors for the Abraham Kuyper Translation Society.

DWIGHT GIBSON

Dwight Gibson is chief exploration officer for The Exploration Group. A veteran international, organizational, and philanthropic strategist, his professional alliances and personal relationships span the globe while his proven exploration methodology delivers on discovery.

Prior to launching The Exploration Group in 2008, Gibson served as senior vice president for Geneva Global, one of the world's leading philanthropy performance advisors. He has served as the North American director and international secretariat of the World Evangelical Alliance and in executive leadership of the Slavic Gospel Association.

Gibson holds an M.A. in broadcasting and philanthropy from Wheaton College Graduate School, an undergraduate degree in communication studies from Indiana Wesleyan University, as well as executive development and management technique certificates from the Johnson School at Cornell University and from the Owens School at Vanderbilt University.

Dwight is an advisory board member of the Billy Graham Center in Wheaton, Illinois; a board chair emeritus of ChinaSource in Fullerton, California, and Hong Kong; and a Sustainable Employment Marketing Committee member, Dow Chemical Michigan Regional Planning Commission, Saginaw, Michigan.

MAKOTO FUJIMURA

Makoto Fujimura is a world-renowned artist, writer, and speaker. His work is exhibited in galleries worldwide. A presidential appointee to the National Council on the Arts from 2003 to 2009, Fujimura served as an international advocate for the arts, speaking with decision makers and advising governmental policies on the arts.

Fujimura has lectured at numerous conferences, universities, and museums, including the Aspen Institute, Yale and Princeton Universities, Sato Museum, and the Phoenix Art Museum. He founded the International Arts Movement, a non-profit that hosts "Encounter" conferences with prominent cultural catalysts.

Fujimura's book, *Refractions: A Journey of Faith, Art and Culture,* is a collection of essays on culture, art, and humanity from people of various backgrounds. For the 400th anniversary of the King James Bible, Crossway Publishing commissioned and published *The Four Holy Gospels*, featuring Fujimura's illuminations of sacred texts. His most recent major mid-career project, *Golden Sea*, encompasses a film, exhibition, and monograph.

DR. TIMOTHY G. ROYER

Timothy Royer is a leader in the study of the autonomic nervous system and has worked to change the treatment paradigm for those with brain-related neurological, physiological, and behavioral issues. Royer founded Neurocore and has led clinical and program development for this eight-clinic operation as well as the Neurocommunity Program. His work has been featured on ESPN and in major publications, including *USA Today, The Los Angeles Times,* and Jim Robbins's breakthrough book, *A Symphony in the Brain.*

Previously, Royer was the division chief of pediatric psychology at Helen DeVos Children's Hospital in Grand Rapids, Michigan. He collaborated with teams of neuropsychologists, neurologists, and behavioral pediatricians to address the cognitive, emotional, and behavioral needs of children.

Royer also served as director of inpatient psychological testing services at Pine Rest, a comprehensive behavioral health center.

Royer holds a Ph.D. in psychology from the Georgia School of Professional Psychology at Argosy University and an M.A. in community counseling from Georgia State University.

EVAN KOONS

Evan Koons is a writer, actor, and maker-of-gratuitous-things. Perhaps best known as the misguided prayer warrior from the *Coffee with Jesus* shorts, Evan has also worked opposite legend Christopher Lloyd (*Back to the Future* series, *Taxi*) in the soon-to-be-released film *The Adventures of Mickey Matson and the Pirate's Code.*

Evan wrote the acclaimed hospice documentary *Except for Six*, a film Ken Burns called "a heartfelt and important film." He has also written a slew of creative projects for non-profits and brands such as T-mobile, Microsoft, and Amazon.com.

Contrary to the film depiction, Evan does not live in the magical land of the farmhouse. Instead, he lives in the magical land of Grand Rapids, Michigan, with his wife, two kids, and their dog, Penelope.

To stay in touch with him and talk all things *For the Life of the World*, you can follow the Twitter account @LettersToExiles and read Evan's blog on LettersToTheExiles.com.

FIELD SIGHTINGS

Check out these key photos from my collection.

We live in a God-created world full of meaning, but how do we figure it all out? Why is a mountain majestic or a gray whale awesome? Have you gazed at the sky, listened to music, or felt the warmth of an embrace, wondering if these experiences pointed to something more? Is our Creator inviting us to know him through our experience of creation? To understand the meaning of everything around us or even about ourselves, we make connections, using things to describe other things. These connections reveal a story and the Author of that story.

I captured some photos on our journey, of things that point to other things. You may want to check them out as you trek through each episode!

House:

Not only is it the place I call home, it is also like the church—the place where heaven and earth meet, a place of offering, communion, rest, and creation. In her, by her, and through her, she is the reminder of God's song, his promises to the world.

Garden:

The field of exile. This is like the world, broken but beautiful and rich, wholly belonging to God.

Plants, Wheel Barrow, Shovel, Rake:

These are the ways we contribute to the care, maintenance, and flourishing of a garden, the tools to seek the welfare of the city of exile.

Bucket of Seed:

This is our investment in the world. We plant seeds for the continued growth and nourishment of our communities. It is a sign and symbol of hope.

Compost Pile:

This is the most basic and natural way we bring nourishment to the garden (or our place in exile). It's messy and can be wearisome to handle, but it's the basis for all healthy growth.

Letter and Pen:

This is my prayer and hope for the people of God. A reminder of our call in God's mission for the world.

Reel-to-Reel Tape Recorder:

A device to preserve the memory of our explorations and discoveries.

Ukulele:

Part muse, part reminder, the ukulele is my song, my contribution to God's *oikonomia*, that is, his economy of all things.

Vintage Movie Cameras:

Camera lenses don't change what exists, but by giving us a new perspective, they help us better make sense of all that exists.

Sheet Music:

Sheet music is one way we record memory: we write it down. It's critical for our understanding and for playing our part in God's purposes. The music must be played!

Art Studio:

The art studio is a place of creativity, where unhindered exploration and stuff-making happens. It's a reminder of God's call on my life (all our lives) to create, work, and give back to the world.

"Fruit of the Tree" Illustration:

A tree can help us understand what it means to give. The purpose of a tree isn't for itself, it's for the life of those around it.

Library:

A place to learn and remember, to grow and rest.

Acorn:

It is a foreshadowing of the oak tree—a sign of our hope in the coming kingdom of God. In the same way, the church is (or should be) the foreshadowing of an eternity with God in heaven.

Porch:

This is a place of rest and contemplation. It leads to the door, which is always open.

Feast Table:

The feast table is a sign of our connection to others through our work. It is a reminder that the work of our hands is first and foremost a communal endeavor.

Chinese Sky Lantern:

Sky lanterns show us our true nature—that we are filled with fire (the Holy Spirit) and offered back to God for his glory.

The Stranger:

The stranger and his accoutrements remind us that justice is nurtured by grace and hospitality. We are reminded to love the stranger as family, because we too are strangers in a strange land. Christ is the stranger. (The world did not know him.)

Bread:

Have you ever thought of bread as a technology, a wondrous demonstration of humankind's ability to combine seemingly disparate stardust and make something new for the benefit all? It reveals the innovative spirit placed in us. It also reveals the depths of God's wisdom and knowledge.

Behold Wine Bottle:

The wine represents God's desire that we take time and engage all of our senses in the wonder and the presence of God. He created all things good. He wants us to take time to experience that goodness and develop a palate for him in all his fullness.

Chess Set:

The chess set represents our ability to see into something, to have insight, to plan and anticipate, to collaborate and create new ideas and technology.

Turtle:

A thing of beauty. Have you ever really looked at a turtle? They're pretty awesome. Just wash your hands when you're done.

Telescope:

This instrument represents God's desire for us to explore the wondrous depths of his creation with the promise that it will reveal more about him and his power and glory.

Invitations:

The invitations are reminders of a party to come—that one day we will celebrate with God forever and ever. The church is the invitation to that party.

HALL OF SCHOLARS

Get wisdom. Get understanding.

Okay, everybody. As we explore our purpose in exile, my t-shirt attire might be a topic for discussion. I wear t-shirts, a lot. In fact, I created a t-shirt series—"Hall of Scholars"—in honor of some keenly helpful trailblazers. So, go ahead. Check out a field scholar and discover each one's unique gifts. You might be inspired to get to know them better on your own. Incidentally, notice a face that does not belong? Maybe it does. Maybe your face belongs, too.

FIELD SCHOLAR: Stephen Grabill

Stephen Grabill is passionate about the harmonizing power of *oikonomia* to merge our lives with God's ultimate purpose for creation and rekindle the church's imagination, as we labor *for the life of the world*. His expertise in economics, theology, and history helps us understand how our stewardship must be rooted in God's big picture for all things.

FIELD SCHOLAR: Alexander Schmemman (1921-1983)

In his book *For the Life of the World*, Alexander Schmemman teaches us that the bedrock of existence is this: all is gift. This core idea helps us understand that God's nature is to give gifts. We bear God's image as gift-givers by offering his gifts back to him and to the world.

FIELD SCHOLAR: Herman Bavinck (1854-1921)

Herman Bavinck was a remarkable authority on family. He explored how God's design for family is the foundation of all society. For a flourishing world, start with a thriving family.

FIELD SCHOLAR: Lester DeKoster (1916 -2012)

Lester DeKoster is known for his thoughts on work. He believed that work is more than a means to personal wealth. Its primary purpose is service to God and service to others.

FIELD SCHOLAR: Abraham Kuyper (1837-1920)

Abraham Kuyper's concept of sphere sovereignty is monumental in understanding justice, order, and breakdown in society. Through Kuyper's exploration of creation, we see the wondrous and unique gifts God grants to every area of life.

FIELD SCHOLAR: Gerard Manley Hopkins (1844-1889)

A Victorian poet and Jesuit priest, Hopkins's poetry reminds us that our pursuit of knowledge and wisdom in the world will reveal more about our creator God. "The world is charged with the grandeur of God," he wrote in "God's Grandeur" (undated poem, c. March–April 1877).

FIELD SCHOLAR: Hans Urs von Balthasar (1905- 1988)

Hans Urs von Balthasar was a scholar and poetic prose writer unparalleled in his contemplation of the good, the beautiful, and the true. His beautifully crafted words tell us that beholding beauty is paramount to communion with God.

FIELD SCHOLAR: Josef Pieper (1904-1997)

In his scholarly work *In Tune with the World: A Theory of Festivity,* Josef Pieper explored how we are created for union with God. We are meant to rest and abide in God both now and forever. In the end of all things, we are told that this looks like a party, a feast.

FIELD SCHOLAR: Evan Koons

Why is my mug included among these erudite scholars? (And why should your face be here, too?) I'm just a dude—a storyteller and artist—wondering and wandering through the world, my faith, and the church.

I dug up the Latin root for the word "scholar" and discovered that *schola* means school. We all are given gifts from God and are called to offer those gifts in service. An essential part of offering our God-given gifts requires seeking knowledge and a deeper relationship with our Creator. The more we know about God and his world, the better we are able to use his gifts as love offerings for others. "Get wisdom. Though it cost all you have, get understanding" (Prov. 4:7). We are created to live as "everyday scholars" in God's world.

EXILE

LETTER FROM EVAN

If you would please ask your group to join me in understanding the nitty-gritty, I would be grateful. Together we will embark on an expedition that might change how we view the world. This journey may even stir deep remembering of forgotten things like expectation and purpose.

Our first episode revisits something so foundational to our Christian walk that it's easy to overlook and misunderstand. God tells us we are exiles, strangers and pilgrims on the earth. Our calling is to a better country, an eternal dwelling. And yet—and here's where it gets tricky—our calling is also *For the Life of the World.*

That means God isn't calling us to a bunker mentality (fortification). He also isn't calling us to dominate the culture around us (domination) or to simply blend in to get along (accommodation).

So how exactly are we supposed to engage the world?

I believe questions, big and small, are essential tools for explorers. Why? Because questions often transform into landmarks on the map of discovery. And those landmarks help us ask better questions that carry us further along our journeys.

In our first episode, we'll explore these questions:

1. What does it mean to be "in the world but not of it"?

2. What is our personal salvation actually for?

3. What does it mean to be the church in exile—welcome "not home"?

How does understanding "all is gift" transform the way we live our daily lives?

FRIENDS ON THE JOURNEY

Dr. Amy Sherman, Writer, Researcher

Amy explains how Christians often view the world and why a new, wider lens is needed. We begin to understand what it means for the church to be in the world but not of it.

Dwight Gibson, Chief Exploration Officer

Dwight discovers the significance of a Chinese sky lantern. His findings reveal how God is "the gift-giver," bestowing gifts on us that we might offer those gifts back to him and others in true exchange.

Dr. Stephen Grabill, Theologian, Scholar

Stephen helps us understand how the church in the world parallels Israel's exile in Babylon. He helps us investigate the difference between the short view and the long view in seeking the welfare of our fellow inhabitants.

THE LANDSCAPE

Fortification, Domination, Accommodation: These are approaches to the world the church has often adopted out of fear rather than love. Instead of embracing the long view—seeking the welfare of the inhabitants of the land we're in—we panic and take the short view. We hide, fight, or blend into our surroundings. The short view is rooted in fear, a reaction to crisis with a sense of urgency.

Babylonian Exile of Israel and the Current Exile of the Church: Israel's exile in Babylon is instrumental in teaching the church how to live in the world but not be of it. The history of Israel and the church reminds us that God's ultimate purpose is restoration.

Oikonomia: This is a Greek term meaning "house management or stewardship." It also helps us understand how each sphere of life—family, work, government, art, education, charities, and more—has its own arrangement or mode of operation. When these spheres blend and interact, it's a grand collaboration that reflects God's *economy of all things*. Oikonomia involves gift exchange in our creative stewardship of culture.

The Song of Gift: We are made in the image of God, called to be gift-givers of the Gift-giver. If we pour out our lives, using our gifts to bless others, we will be blessed in return (though not necessarily in material ways). This communal blessing produces abundance and flourishing.

The Welfare of the City: The Israelites were commanded to seek the welfare of the city in their place of exile. The church is also called to seek the welfare of the earth's inhabitants during our pilgrimage here. This is our priestly calling as gift-givers in God's economy of all things.

STUDIO WORK | *IDEA EXCHANGE*

1. Have you experienced or adopted the *fortification*, *domination*, or *accommodation* approaches in your church?

   What is the root cause of these three responses to the world?

2. Do you view your salvation solely as a means of being rescued from sin?

   Do you think God has a purpose for his children on earth, beyond personal salvation and the personal salvation of others? If yes, how does this perspective play out in your daily life? How does your daily life contribute to the welfare of your community?

3. The Israelites are exiled in Babylon for disobeying the Lord, but the Lord promises to restore them to their homeland after a generation has passed. Jeremiah explains to Israel's leaders that, in the mean time, they are to seek the welfare of the city where they now live. In a sense, they are called to bloom where they are planted (Jer. 29:7). What will happen if they do?

   How does seeking the welfare of the city work toward God's ultimate purpose and Israel's future?

4. Why do we forget we are strangers in a strange land, not home yet?

   Does the long-view perspective of the church in exile transform how we engage our surroundings?

5. In God's economy of all things, his oikonomia, is your daily labor solely a means to provide for yourself, your family, your church, and maybe your favorite charitable cause?

   For what purpose is your work designed? What is your economic responsibility? How might you grow your God-given gifts in order to enlarge your vision to serve others in need of your gifts?

6. Have we forgotten to be gift-givers in all our relationships and exchanges?

How has our calling as gift-givers, as a royal priesthood, been restored? And for what purpose has our calling been restored? (What is your salvation actually for?)

7. How is a Chinese sky lantern a good metaphor for our lives, our work, our gifts?

How is our work connected to the earth in the places we live? Do we seek to serve locally, nationally, globally?

PORCH STEPS | *HELLO WORLD*

1. The prophet Jeremiah buys a field and buries the deed (Jer. 29–33). His actions are rooted in the promise that God will lead Israel back to its homeland. Jeremiah knew the return would not happen in his lifetime, yet he acted for the benefit of those who would come after him. How might you "bury the deed" in the various "fields" to which you have been called, even though you may not see the benefits in your lifetime? Do you view your gift-giving as a calling to serve in the specific locations where God has placed you?

2. How does understanding *all is gift* change the way you approach your daily work and interactions with others? Is your work a heavenward offering? What are the ways you might carry out the calling to be a royal priesthood, to bless others with the gifts God has blessed you?

3. How do you define success or your purpose in life? Is it connected to the welfare of the city where you have been placed? What would it take to transform your city?

4. What does it mean to "prepare the way of the Lord"? What are some ways you could do this in the specific location God has placed you?

LANTERN LIGHT

Isaiah 55:11 ... *so is my word that goes out from my mouth: It will not return to me empty, but will accomplish what I desire and achieve the purpose for which I sent it.*

Entangled in the everyday grind of life in exile, I sometimes lose sight of a staggering, awe-inspiring reality: I have a God-breathed book I can open every day for strength and wisdom. The story of exile is woven throughout Scripture. The Pentateuch, prophetic books, wisdom books, historical chronicles, and New Testament all speak to us about our journey on earth and illuminate God's purpose for his creation. We read, we meditate on these living words, and by the power of the Holy Spirit we grow in grace as the living body of Christ in the world. So I hope you'll join me in reading these Scripture selections as we journey together. We'll learn more about God's everlasting love for us and his plans for the flourishing of his handiwork.

Psalm 24:1–2 *The earth is the Lord's ...*

Jeremiah 29:7 *Seek the peace and prosperity of the city ...*

Jeremiah 29:11 *'For I know the plans I have for you,' declares the Lord, 'plans to prosper you ...'*

Jeremiah 29–33 Israel's exile in Babylon

Hebrews 11:1 *Now faith is confidence in what we hope for and assurance about what we do not see.*

Hebrews 11:13 *... admitting that they were foreigners and strangers on earth.*

Ephesians 2:10 *For we are God's handiwork, created in Christ Jesus to do good works ...*

1 Peter 1:17 *... live out your time as foreigners here in reverent fear.*

PRAYER JOURNAL

1. Thank you, Jesus, for the gift of your life, for restoring our communion with God and renewing our calling as gift-givers. Through your perfect sacrifice you have given us the power to love and bless others with our gifts. My heart rejoices.

2. Father God, I need wisdom to know how to use the gifts you have given me, *for the life of the world.* You promise to give wisdom to all who ask. Knowing that your ultimate purpose is restoration fills me with hope and expectation. Thank you.

READ MORE

Stewardship Study Bible. Grand Rapids: Zondervan, 2009, pp. x–xii.

Kingdom Stewardship. Edited by Arif Mohamed, Brett Elder, and Stephen Grabill. Grand Rapids: Christian's Library Press, 2010, pp. 7–16.

Berghoef, Gerard, and DeKoster, Lester. *Faithful in All God's House: Stewardship and the Christian Life.* Grand Rapids: Christian's Library Press, 2013, pp. 7–22.

EP2 LOVE

EPISODE TWO:

ECONOMY OF LOVE

LETTER FROM EVAN

In this episode, we will meet some fellow strangers in a strange land who reflect on their unique journeys into f-a-m-i-l-y. Multitudinous definitions for love, marriage, family, and community pile up like options on a menu. Is there an original design or purpose we have forgotten? Why did God create the family? Let's explore a true and ancient source—the Bible.

We'll go all the way back to the beginning and investigate:

1. For what purpose did God create male and female, and how does this design express the nature of the Trinity?

2. How is family design created for gift-giving, for abundance? When you say *yes* to marriage and family, what are you saying *yes* to?

3. How does family life help us find our true nature, created in God's image? How does this affect our response to the world?

FRIENDS ON THE JOURNEY

Dr. Amy Sherman, Writer, Researcher

Amy discusses her love for compost. This messy, earthy stuff provides a foundation for growth in a garden much like messy, earthy family life provides the foundation for growth in society. She helps us contemplate the characteristics of the first family, the Holy Family, and Jesus' family tree (which looks surprisingly similar to many families).

Dwight Gibson, Chief Exploration Officer

Dwight treks the great unknown in search of an ideal family. He discovers how daily, faithful steps of ordinary family life contribute to the welfare of the city.

The Zwyghuizen Family, a.k.a. Team Z

Team Z shares how their family story plays a role in God's larger story. In living out their family motto—encouraging, loving, and blessing—they offer their family gifts, *for the life of the world.*

THE LANDSCAPE

God's Design for the Family: Family design reflects the nature of the Trinity, pouring out abundance for the life of the world.

Saying Yes: In saying *yes* to your beloved, to marriage, to family, we say *yes* to walking by faith and living a life of offering, our priestly calling to be gift-givers in the world.

Foundations of Family and the Foundations of Society: Healthy, flourishing families create healthy, flourishing societies by providing loving and supportive environments for growth.

Healthy Soil: All of life starts with healthy soil. Healthy soil nourishes plants. Loving families that seek to bless their communities create abundance for those living around them.

STUDIO WORK | *IDEA EXCHANGE*

1. How does our culture define marriage and family?

   Do these definitions vary with God's design and purpose for family? How do you approach others who have different views of family? Do you criticize, avoid topics, or tell people to do what is right in their own eyes? What is a God-glorifying response to non-Christian views about family and relationships?

2. Is marriage more than a contract?

   The church often behaves the same as secular culture regarding sex, marriage, and family. We blend in. Do we understand the deeper meaning of marriage and the purpose God has designed for family? Have you thought of your family as a blessing to be shared for the welfare of those around you?

3. How is compost similar to family?

   How does family design contribute to flourishing in the places we live? As a family, do you keep to yourself, or do you enter "the city" and encounter those who do not share your faith?

4. No one has seen God, and no one can fully fathom the Trinity. "For the foolishness of God is wiser than human wisdom, and the weakness of God is stronger than human strength" (I Cor. 1:25). Our finite metaphor for the Trinity in this episode—three beings joyfully and perfectly completing each other, pouring out love and creative power in the creation of a family—underscores the inability of our minds to fully comprehend an indescribably infinite God. A God who is complete in himself. Yet God desires that we know him, and one day we will see him face to face.

As we seek to know our Creator, for what purpose did he make us male and female? And what is the nature of the Trinity that is reflected in family? Does the church live as a reflection of the Trinity?

5. How does God work through the church to transform the world?

Is the accommodation approach similar to putting your gift of salvation under a bowl? Matthew 5:16 says, "let your light shine before others, that they may see your good deeds and glorify your Father in heaven."

6. How is family unromantic, humble, or even the "school of love"?

How is the entire church a family? How might the church as a family be "pointed out" to bless the world with unique gifts, expressed freely and creatively?

7. Why did Jesus enter our spiritual exile and identify with us as human beings?

How are we to be his hands and feet, extensions of his love and sacrifice in the world? 1 Corinthians 12:27 says: "Now you are the body of Christ, and each one of you is a part of it."

PORCH STEPS | *HELLO WORLD*

1. What is a healthy family, a healthy soil? What attitudes and habits create flourishing for those around you for the long term? How do we unwittingly limit the positive growth of gifts? Do you nourish others with encouragement and love, by the power of God's truth; and how will this "prepare the way of the Lord" as we live our lives on earth?

2. What does "one step at a time" look like in your life? How are the small picture and the big picture a part of the same story in God's purposes? What are some small, everyday steps you might take in your life to be *pointed out* as a blessing for others?

3. Do you actively think of how you might share or "pour out" your family for the life of the world?

LANTERN LIGHT

Genesis 2:15–25 *It is not good for the man to be alone. I will make a helper suitable for him.*

Psalm 68:6 *God sets the lonely in families …*

Matthew 1 *This is the genealogy of Jesus the Messiah …*

Mark 10:6–9 *But at the beginning of creation God 'made them male and female.'*

Luke 1:46–55 Mary's song *His mercy extends to those who fear him, from generation to generation …*

PRAYER JOURNAL

1. Thank you, Father, that you work all things for good in the lives of your children and powerfully use our families to bless the world with your gifts.

2. Lord, I want to live *pointed out* as a blessing to others. Family life can be a mundane and messy business. I ask for eyes and ears that are sensitive to the needs of those you have placed in my life.

READ MORE

Ballor, Jordan J. *Get Your Hands Dirty: Essays on Christian Social Thought (and Action)*. Eugene, Ore.: Wipf & Stock, 2013, pp. 1–45.

Bavinck, Herman. *The Christian Family.* Translated by Nelson D. Kloosterman. Edited by Stephen J. Grabill. Grand Rapids: Christian's Library Press, 2012, pp. 63–86, 109–34.

EP3 CREATIVE SERVICE

ECONOMY OF CREATIVE SERVICE

LETTER FROM EVAN

Does the word "economy" fill your mind with images of a cold, impersonal machine, an unwieldy nest of levers and gears crammed with people trying to survive? What if the world's economy was something much more personal, something beautiful and mysterious in its vastness? Perhaps our daily work is a call to reflect an infinitely creative God.

In this episode, we'll explore the goodness of work. That's right. Work is a gift. It was not always tangled with thorns and thistles. Glimmers of its original purpose cast an unmistakable glow through our creative service.

We'll roll up our sleeves and ponder:

1. Is work merely about utility, efficiency, and progress? What is the role of our work in God's economy of all things?

2. How does our individual creative work contribute to a greater whole? What is "the great collaboration"?

3. Is work impersonal or personal? Is it communal? How does it shape us?

FRIENDS ON THE JOURNEY

Dr. Stephen Grabill, Theologian, Scholar

Stephen explains how work is not merely for survival and gain. Work is a gift from God to shape us and to bless others.

Dwight Gibson, Chief Exploration Officer

Dwight reads a story about an unusual tree to a young audience. This particular tree exhibits shocking behavior.

The Little Acorn Kids

An astute roundtable discussion provides instructive insight on the difference between giving and "un-giving." And someone chomps an apple while contemplating a question: What is the true nature of a tree?

THE LANDSCAPE

We Are Makers: A part of what it means to be made in God's image is to be a maker like him.

Work as Calling: Each of us has been created for a purpose, to fulfill a key role in serving others with the gifts and talents God has given us.

Value in the Exchange: Value is created when we freely exchange our gifts with one another as an act of blessing.

Creative Collaboration: We create more than consumable products and services. We play a part in the divine project of creativity. In creating relationships with countless others in a vast collaboration, we meet each other's needs and desires.

STUDIO WORK | *IDEA EXCHANGE*

1. How does *work* work in God's economy of all things?

   Is our work all about the American dream, about personal success and upward mobility?

2. How is our communal nature demonstrated by our gift nature? What does this look like?

   How do our personal callings operate in this framework, this vast collaboration? Should collaboration remain within the church, or should it involve our communities? Would it depend on the collaboration?

3. How does the "Un-giving Tree" help us understand what work isn't?

   How might the tree's behavior bear resemblance to the fortification approach to the world? Does this approach or lifestyle reflect God's glory and his gifts to the world?

4. Did God create us for work?

   How has work changed after Adam and Eve fell away from God in the Garden of Eden? How has man-centered or self-centered work (rather than God-centered, God-glorifying work) affected the world around us?

5. How many hands, or roles, are employed in making the craftsman table?

How do individuals freely collaborate with their God-given gifts to meet community needs and desires? Are relationships inherently personal and local? How deeply do these relationships grow?

6. What is the *oikonomia* of economics, the great collaboration in our work? What does it mean to profit? How is wealth and profit a God-given responsibility? In Deuteronomy 8:17–18, God reminds the Israelites that all is a gift from him. What does this responsibility require of us? How does the parable of the talents (Matt. 25:14–30) relate to Deuteronomy 8:17–18?

Seeking the welfare of the city implies abundant living, where we enjoy God's creation beyond mere daily survival. Civilizations flourish through increase. Our work must create a profit, an increase, which enables us to bless others. Increase also grants us time to appreciate God's world as we work in his garden. If our creative endeavors build and make more than we need from day to day, we are able to meet needs as well as desires (1 Cor. 3:7–9).

Is there profit in seeking the welfare of the city and incorporating the long-term view? Or is value created with short-term goals, a quick turnaround?

7. What happens if people are allowed to offer their gifts to one another in free and open exchange?

What happens to creativity if the process is largely controlled?

PORCH STEPS | *HELLO WORLD*

1. Do you toil merely to tend to your body, to your family? If work is a gift for others, how does this change the way we do our daily labor? How does a "personal survival" attitude about work affect the "cities" in which we live?

2. How might we seek justice in areas where there is exploitation? How does wisdom and virtue transform the way we exchange our gifts? Do you view other people as gift-bearers?

3. How do our possessions reveal the gifts of others? Are we alone, surviving by our own wits? Are you involved in the collaborations taking place at work and in the areas where you live? What does Proverbs 31:13–20 tell us about work and profit? This passage seems to suggest that flourishing entails productivity: productive activities generate new things and lead to a profit. Describe the connection in Proverbs 31 between flourishing, productivity, and profit.

LANTERN LIGHT

Psalm 104:24 *How many are your works, Lord! In wisdom you made them all …*

Jeremiah 29:5 *Build houses and settle down; plant gardens and eat what they produce.*

Luke 12:22–23 *… life is more than food, and the body more than clothes …*

Philippians 2:3–4 *Do nothing out of selfish ambition or vain conceit. Rather, in humility value others above yourselves …*

Colossians 3:23 *Whatever you do, work at it with all your heart …*

PRAYER JOURNAL

1. Thank you, Father, that I am not alone, and that my needs and desires are supplied by the gifts you have given through the work and service of others.

2. Lord, help me to remember that my work is personal and relational. Your plan for creative service—a vast collaboration designed for flourishing and the welfare of those around me—reaches far beyond my imagination.

READ MORE

Bolt, John. *Economic Shalom: A Reformed Primer on Faith, Work, and Human Flourishing.* Grand Rapids: Christian's Library Press, 2013, pp. 25–40.

Brand, Chad. *Flourishing Faith: A Baptist Primer on Work, Economics, and Civic Stewardship.* Grand Rapids: Christian's Library Press, 2012, pp. 11–44.

DeKoster, Lester. *Work: The Meaning of Your Life.* 2d ed. Grand Rapids: Christian's Library Press, 2010.

Self, Charlie. *Flourishing Churches and Communities: A Pentecostal Primer on Faith, Work, and Economics for Spirit-Empowered Discipleship.* Grand Rapids: Christian's Library Press, 2013, pp. 45–67.

Wright, David. *How God Makes the World a Better Place: A Wesleyan Primer on Faith, Work, and Economic Transformation.* Grand Rapids: Christian's Library Press, 2012, pp. 1–16.

EP4 ORDER

ECONOMY OF ORDER

LETTER FROM EVAN

In a fallen world, the song of 'all is gift' often grows faint and obscure. We spurn justice, abundance dwindles, and dysfunction mars a once perfect creation. Romans 8:19–23 says creation groans. What causes all of the hurt and disorder in our places of exile? What or who can help heal the brokenness? When we try to fix the breakdown of God's perfect order with ill-fitting (though well-meaning) contraptions, it's painfully evident that creativity suffers and wanes. In God's economy of all things, how does creativity, freedom, and justice work together toward flourishing and restoration?

In this episode, we'll play some hockey and thoroughly knock about these questions as well as a few more:

1. What is a code of honor, and how does it maintain balance? What is a "managed game," and why is it boring?

2. Do gardeners make plants grow, or do they cultivate the conditions for growth?

3. What role does hospitality play in God's economy of order? How is hospitality essential for justice to thrive?

4. Who is the "stranger," and who is the "face of justice"?

FRIENDS ON THE JOURNEY

Dr. Stephen Grabill, Theologian, Scholar

Stephen exchanges his scholarly robes for a hockey uniform. When hockey players police themselves and follow a code of honor, the game is as it should be—exciting. But sometimes players abandon the code and referees have to step in to restore order.

Dr. Anthony Bradley, Associate Professor of Theology & Ethics

Anthony blows a whistle on power and corruption. He explains how dysfunction chokes flourishing when we abandon our true work as gardeners in God's economy of order.

Dwight Gibson, Chief Exploration Officer

Dwight leaves a small package containing big thoughts on justice and hospitality. These two words could change how you view strangers.

Dr. John Perkins, Theologian & Freedom Activist

John explains how honoring the image of God in each person affirms each one's God-given dignity and cultivates human flourishing: "We don't give dignity. We affirm it."

THE LANDSCAPE

Code of Honor: Justice is the fuel that powers a creative, exciting game. When players voluntarily follow the rules of the game, the experience becomes an adventure, rather than a boring, worn path.

Cultivation: As gardeners, we have a provocative role: we set up the garden for flourishing. Each plant is placed where it might reach its full potential.

Order of Economies: Art, government, education, family, and business are economies, spheres of God's creation with their own arrangements and modes of operation.

Justice & Hospitality: Hospitality is justice in action. Justice needs a face. That face looks a lot like the church offering hospitality to the stranger. We cast fear aside and tell the stranger: "I love you. I honor you. You are significant. You are made in God's image." Loving the stranger is not a program that a government or organization can make happen. It takes individuals willing to enter into the lives of other individuals.

The Stranger: Christ came into the world and we did not know him. We were estranged from God, and yet, Christ gave his life for us, to restore communion with our Creator. In the same way, we are called to give ourselves away for the sake of the stranger because Christ is the Stranger.

STUDIO WORK | *IDEA EXCHANGE*

1. What situations or events lead to a managed game, and what kind of impact does this management have on creativity and flourishing?

   How might our God-given gifts and creativity languish in a cookie-cutter approach to serving others?

2. How does a gardener have a provocative role in setting up the garden?

How are we to be gardeners in our places of exile, seeking the welfare of those around us? How well would a gardener have to know or understand the plants, the soil, and the geography of the garden in order to cultivate an environment for flourishing? How would a managed game hinder this organic gardening process?

3. What causes the breakdown of God's economy of order (Ezek. 22:29)? What is hospitality all about, and why is it necessary for maintaining a society where justice prevails (Deut. 10:19)?

Does fear hinder you from being hospitable to strangers? What is behind our fear of the stranger, and how does that fear impact our surroundings? Would seeking friendship with strangers help you know your community's needs and be a means for restoring order to broken places (Lev. 19:34)?

4. What does the marionette performance teach us about mercy and grace to the stranger?

What does it mean to live "in accordance with the gift of mercy and grace which we have received ourselves"? What does it mean to have your life ransomed?

5. Are we to be hospitable only to the household of faith (Gal. 6:10)?

Do you connect or engage with people that enter your daily life? Do you keep your relationship-building inside Christian communities?

6. How is each person's dignity a glorious, creative, capable gift to the world?

Who is "the Stranger"? Who are some strangers you have encountered in your life? Did you meet the opportunity, or did you pass it by?

7. "I will put my Spirit on him, and he will bring justice to the nations" (Isa. 42:1). What does it mean to see "with the eyes of Christ"? What will we see?

Christ called the church his beloved and sought us while we were lost. Do we seek out strangers with the love of Christ?

PORCH STEPS | *HELLO WORLD*

1. Are we able to give another human being dignity? How do Christians "do justice"? When you reach out to individuals—the stranger—do you try to force them to fit into the Christian cultural mold, or do you point them to Christ?

2. How might you welcome and make space for the stranger in your life (Matt. 25:35)? If we invite the stranger, the poor, the widow, and the orphan into our homes and churches, how does this create a just society? How does knowing the stranger transform our environments (Rom. 12:13)? Are you cautious of people who appear different or behave differently from you, or do you connect with a variety of people?

3. Does seeking order and justice require designing a new and improved system, or are they found in God's original plans and design? How might you help the downtrodden in your communities discover their unique gifts and offer them for the life of the world?

LANTERN LIGHT

Leviticus 19:33–34 *The foreigner residing among you must be treated as your native-born. Love them as yourself …*

Jeremiah 29:13–14 *You will seek me and find me when you seek me with all your heart.*

Isaiah 42:1 *I will put my Spirit on him, and he will bring justice to the nations.*

Luke 14:12–14 *When you give a banquet, invite the poor, the crippled, the lame, the blind, and you will be blessed.*

Romans 5:8 *But God demonstrates his own love for us in this: While we were still sinners, Christ died for us.*

Hebrews 13:2 *Do not forget to show hospitality to strangers, for by so doing some people have shown hospitality to angels without knowing it.*

PRAYER JOURNAL

1. Father, thank you that the earth is full of your creative order and redemptive love. Dignity is a gift of grace, your image in us, not something we must earn (for we are not able). When we are weak, you are strong and mighty to restore order.

2. Lord, grant me the power to live a life of hospitality, to share your love with those who bear your image.

READ MORE

Brand, Chad. *Flourishing Faith: A Baptist Primer on Work, Economics, and Civic Stewardship.* Grand Rapids: Christian's Library Press, 2012, pp. 45–69.

Kuyper, Abraham. *Guidance for Christian Engagement in Government.* Translated and edited by Harry Van Dyke. Grand Rapids: CLP Academic, 2013, pp. 39–70.

Wright, David. *How God Makes the World a Better Place: A Wesleyan Primer on Faith, Work, and Economic Transformation.* Grand Rapids: Christian's Library Press, 2012, pp. 89–108.

ECONOMY OF WISDOM

LETTER FROM EVAN

Psalm 111:10 tells us that the starting point for wisdom is "the fear of the Lord." What does that mean, exactly? Everywhere, you see and hear: knowledge is power. But how does knowledge mingle with wisdom? Are they different?

In this episode, we will explore the profundity of knowing.

1. Knowledge is power, but more than that.

2. Knowledge sees beyond scarcity and reveals abundance.

3. Knowledge unleashes human potential.

4. Knowledge helps us love better.

5. Knowledge becomes wisdom when it remembers the Creator.

FRIENDS ON THE JOURNEY

Dr. Stephen Grabill, Theologian, Scholar

We discover that a chef's hat suits Stephen quite well. His bread baking skills reveal an awesome possession of the human intellect—fire. God gives us the ability to transform the stuff of the earth into abundance; knowledge as insight creates flourishing.

Dwight Gibson, Chief Exploration Officer

Dwight gets his head examined at a brain studio. He discovers afresh that "we are fearfully and wonderfully made" (Ps. 139:14).

Dr. Tim Royer, NeuroCore (A Brain Studio)

Tim shares an astounding scientific thought: "It has been estimated that there are more neuronal connections in our brains than there are stars in the entire universe." We visit a classroom to investigate potential.

THE LANDSCAPE

Human Intellect: God created us with the ability for insight, to *see into* his creation. With this knowledge, we create abundance and serve others. This is our priestly calling.

Scarcity: Knowledge used for selfish power and gain produces scarcity rather than abundance.

Shared Knowledge: When knowledge is shared, it grows. It never becomes less. Knowledge informed by God's truth creates flourishing.

Individual Potential: God created us as individuals with different and complementary gifts. Discovering and nurturing this creative potential for service, for blessing others, is our calling.

Knowledge & Wisdom: Knowledge leads to wisdom when used with love—mirroring our Creator.

STUDIO WORK | *IDEA EXCHANGE*

1. Is knowledge about power and dominion, or something more?

   In God's economy of wisdom, what do we use knowledge for? How might pride overshadow grace in our knowledge of God and his creation? How does prideful knowledge manifest itself in relationships or service?

2. What is the human intellect and how may it be used for blessing?

   Was your mind created to store facts and use knowledge as a barrier to suffering and a sinful world?

3. What does it meant to "see into" God's creation?

   Does this involve our creativity as God's image-bearers? In our places of exile, how might we use our God-given insight to bless our neighbors?

4. What happens when you share knowledge?

   Is it better to share knowledge with fellow church members or anyone that God brings into your life? Do you share knowledge as a gift, an exciting discovery you can't wait to pass on? Do you share discoveries even though you may not see the benefits in your lifetime?

5. How do we recognize and cultivate the potential for each individual to mirror our Creator? Psalm 139:14 tells us that we are "fearfully and wonderfully made." In ancient Hebrew, *fearfully* means "with great interest, heartfelt interest and respect," and *wonderfully* is translated as "unique, set apart, uniquely marvelous." What do these words tell us about God and how he creates us as individuals?

Does your church know its members well enough to understand or appreciate unique or individual gifts? How might those gifts harmonize to bless your community?

6. How does knowledge lead to wisdom?

Is God's creation governed by scarcity or abundance? Is complete self-sufficiency elevated as a virtue in scripture?

7. As we explore God's world, how does his creation reveal who he is? Are things in the world signs of something else?

Why is it important to say, "Fire is like God," rather than, "God is like fire"? In your community, who or what is recognized as the source of life, material and spiritual? Is God the I AM, through Jesus the Logos (Word), viewed as the Creator and source of all life? John 1:3 says: "Through him all things were made ..." Should we ask God for wisdom about the future? How might the church in exile share our hope of restoration?

PORCH STEPS | *HELLO WORLD*

1. Do you share knowledge, all that you have learned in your life, for blessing others? If you share what you know, how might that knowledge grow to produce abundance and flourishing? Is sharing knowledge important to you?

2. How might we nurture the individual gifts of people in our lives and help them be who they were created to be? How might those unique gifts bless the communities where you live? If we use our gifts to the fullest potential in service to others, how would this affect a community? What elements or attitudes in a culture could hinder unique gifts from blossoming?

3. What are some ways we might seek to know God by discovering more about his creation? Do we eagerly and creatively explore God's creation because "the more we know, the more we may bless"? Do you fear scarcity?

LANTERN LIGHT

Psalm 139:14 *I praise you because I am fearfully and wonderfully made; your works are wonderful, I know that full well.*

Proverbs 3:19 *By wisdom the Lord laid the earth's foundations, by understanding he set the heavens in place …*

Proverbs 4:6–7 *The beginning of wisdom is this: Get wisdom …*

Philippians 2:13 *… for it is God who works in you to will and to act in order to fulfill his good purpose.*

James 1:5 *If any of you lacks wisdom, you should ask God, who gives generously to all without finding fault, and it will be given to you.*

James 3:17 *But the wisdom that comes from heaven is first of all pure, then peace-loving, considerate, submissive, full of mercy and good fruit, impartial and sincere.*

PRAYER JOURNAL

1. Father, I am thankful for the many talents and rich potential you have planted in each of us. With your abundant gifts we can work together, meeting needs with the fire of creative insight.

2. Lord, help us to seek you with all our heart, soul, and mind. Establish a holy hunger for learning in our lives. And may our discoveries be conduits of your healing wisdom in the world.

READ MORE

Kuyper, Abraham. *Scholarship: Two Convocation Addresses on University Life.* Translated by Harry Van Dyke. Grand Rapids: Christian's Library Press, 2014.

Kuyper, Abraham. *Wisdom & Wonder: Common Grace in Science & Art.* Translated by Nelson D. Kloosterman. Edited by Jordan J. Ballor and Stephen J. Grabill. Grand Rapids: Christian's Library Press, 2011, pp. 31–104.

EP6 WONDER

ECONOMY OF WONDER

LETTER FROM EVAN

. . . .

I think I may be losing my ability to wonder. Honestly, it invites a little panic. Enclosed in a world with only a mirror of myself, the solitude is crushing.

What does wonder require? What happens to your heart, mind, and body? Do you have to be somewhere, or is it a perspective that is possible anywhere?

Let's take an unpractical moment to contemplate:

1. How placing ourselves at the center of the universe (self-centeredness) blinds us to the mysterious beauty and wonder in God's creation.

2. How wonder helps us develop a palate for what is good. What does it mean to "taste and see that the Lord is good" (Ps. 34:8)?

3. How beauty and wonder lead us beyond man-made control, beyond human imagination, to an infinitely creative God who calls us on a mysterious, adventurous quest to know him. This is our priestly calling in the world. (In philosophical jargon, "wastefulness" and "uselessness" are the opposites of cold efficiency and pragmatism. Beauty and wonder surpass the confines of practicality.)

FRIENDS ON THE JOURNEY

Dr. Stephen Grabill, Theologian, Scholar

Stephen asks me to taste a book on wine making. Really, actually taste it. Knowledge without wonder and appreciation is pretty dry and tasteless. Wonder and appreciation make wine making something to behold.

Mako Fujimura, Fine Artist

A visit to Fujimura's art studio helps us understand what it means to *behold*. We learn God's love is not merely transactional. It is gratuitous, extravagant beauty.

Evan, The Child

I think I'll spend the day doing something useless, a decision that beckons me to become like a child (Matt. 18:3). Follow me.

THE LANDSCAPE

Narcissism: Self-focused rather than God-focused wonder.

Behold: To wonder at the beauty, abundance, and truth within God's creation.

Pragmatism: Assessing value based on practical usefulness and efficiency.

Waste & Uselessness: Philosophical terms for things that are not utilitarian. Wonder appreciates the value of things in and of themselves, not their pragmatic value.

Wonder & Wisdom: Wonder is to wisdom what flavor is to cooking. "Taste and see that the Lord is good" (Ps. 34:8).

Extravagant Beauty: God sent his Son to die for us while we were sinners estranged from him (Rom. 5:8). His wondrous, extravagant love restored us to himself, to his truth and beauty. Because of his love, we have the gift of wonder—to know him.

STUDIO WORK | *IDEA EXCHANGE*

1. Stephen tosses these nuggets of conventional wisdom to Evan: "Be true to the god within you. Just do it. Have it your way. You deserve it." What viewpoint or focus propels these attitudes?

   Is it ideal to have a world that focuses entirely on you? Is it possible for church culture and families to be too inward focused? How might we share the wonder of God's creation with others in our various places of exile?

2. What does Evan mean when he says he is going to do something totally useless?

   Does church culture take time for beauty? Are church programs measured by human—that is, man-centered—measurements of efficiency and accomplishment? If we took time to bask in God's creation, to wonder at his love and faithfulness, how might those outside the church be affected? How would it benefit those in the church? Does your church measure members by their usefulness to the church?

3. Balthasar wrote, "Those who sneer at the name of beauty will no longer be able to pray or love ..." Why?

How might trying to be useful emphasize a reliance on our own strength rather than on God's power? How would relying on human wisdom and strength make the church "of the world" rather than "in the world"?

4. What is the importance of wonder (to appreciate the value that things have in and of themselves)?

Why do we always want to assign a pragmatic use for things? Does a baby have value? Do we value people for good looks and accomplishments, or do human beings have intrinsic value because God made us in his image? Do you value people for what they can do for you, or for who they are, made in God's image?

5. What does knowledge apart from appreciation taste like?

What does it mean to "taste and see that the Lord is good"? In our busy culture, driven by usefulness, do we rest in the finished work of Jesus? Do we taste the sweet fruit of our bond in Christ, or does the church try to prove its worth in the world? Do we share the exhilarating restfulness of wonder with those outside the church?

6. What will happen if we lose a sense of the goodness and wonder of what God has made?

Why would the word "behold" appear hundreds of times in Scripture? In sheltering ourselves from negative cultural impacts, do we forget to express joy in God's creation or share wonderful discoveries with the inhabitants of the "city"?

7. Do you see beauty in the Gospel?

How is the ability to wonder and appreciate God's beauty a priestly calling in the world? How has our ability to *behold* been affected by the fall? How would beholding God's beauty transform our hearts and help us share God's truth in our communities?

PORCH STEPS | *HELLO WORLD*

1. Do you believe the church has exiled—or removed—beauty from its conversations? Why? How does rediscovering the importance of beauty affect the welfare of the city? How might you introduce a conversation about beauty with a neighbor?

2. How do you value your surroundings and those people around you? Do you take time to wonder at God's creation? Do you assign a "usefulness" value to everything in your life? How might this develop into an attitude of dominating or controlling your surroundings?

3. Why do we need to tell the story of God's beauty when pragmatism and utility become overbearing? Is beauty merely transactional? Is the gospel transactional? How does *gospel beauty*, the story of God's gratuitous, extravagant love, affect your relationships both in and outside church walls?

LANTERN LIGHT

Genesis 1:31 *God saw all that he had made, and it was very good.*

Psalm 40:5 *Many, Lord my God, are the wonders you have done, the things you planned for us. None can compare with you ...*

Psalm 27:4 *... this only do I seek: that I may dwell in the house of the Lord all the days of my life, to gaze on the beauty of the Lord and to seek him in his temple.*

Mark 14 Mary of Bethany *'Leave her alone,' said Jesus. 'Why are you bothering her? She has done a beautiful thing to me.'*

John 1:3 *Through him all things were made; without him nothing was made that has been made.*

PRAYER JOURNAL

1. Thank you, Father, that we are valued by your extravagant love and not by our usefulness. Thank you for the gift of wonder that we might seek you and know you.

2. Please, Lord, give us an appetite for what is good, beautiful, and true. Help us to behold your creation with your perfect love.

READ MORE

Kuyper, Abraham. *Wisdom & Wonder: Common Grace in Science & Art.* Translated by Nelson D. Kloosterman. Edited by Jordan J. Ballor and Stephen J. Grabill. Grand Rapids: Christian's Library Press, 2011, pp. 105–82.

EP7 CHURCH

THE CHURCH

LETTER FROM EVAN

Friends and strangers, we have traveled far on our quest to discover what it means to be *in the world, not of it*. Love. Creative Service. Order. Wisdom. Wonder. The everlasting melody *all is gift* resonates in all of God's economies. Oikonomia is the music we play in our diverse and complementary callings, harmonizing in the house management of God's creation.

As a royal priesthood, our call is to be salt and light. In our daily tasks and creative collaborations we offer God's gifts for the life of the world; and God transforms us and our surroundings through our labor in every sphere of culture.

Yet, I find myself asking, will this *not home* feeling have an end? Is there a loving purpose behind it all? This is the last episode, but not the end of the story. I think we are ready to grasp the riches of *anamnesis* and *prolepsis*, heavy-duty concepts that shed light on God's story for the world. The meaning of these words might even rekindle the gift of creative vision.

1. How do we remember the music of oikonomia? What is anamnesis? Does the church journey in the world as a *lived memory*?

2. What does the church have to do with an acorn? What is prolepsis? And how should we live in the *not yet now*?

3. How is our individual and collaborative work in exile interwoven in God's plan for all things? What is the "Song of Zion"?

FRIENDS ON THE JOURNEY

Dr. Stephen Grabill, Theologian, Scholar

Stephen explains prolepsis, the *not yet now* of an acorn, and what this metaphor holds for the church in exile. He reminds us that anamnesis is the lived memory of God's purposes in the world: "The church is the body of Christ given as a gift for the life of the world."

People at the Feast

Suddenly, gift-givers start arriving, one after another, after another, after another. They transform my garden into something I never imagined. It looks very much like preparation for something—for Someone.

THE LANDSCAPE

Anamnesis: The lived memory. The church is the lived memory of God's purposes in the world.

Prolepsis: The *not yet now* of the coming kingdom of God. Our daily lives lived in the now are continually participating in God's unfolding purposes for the life of the world.

The Acorn: Inside an acorn, the oak tree already is. It is metaphor for prolepsis, the *not yet now* of the kingdom of God.

The Church: The church is the body of Christ given as a gift for the life of the world. In preparing the way of the Lord into the world of exile, we prepare ourselves for him.

Song of Zion: As the Israelites sang for their return to Jerusalem, so too, the church sings the song of promised renewal for all of creation, the fulfillment of God's kingdom come.

The Wedding Feast of the Lamb: In Revelation 19:6, Jesus promises to return for his church in the restoration of all creation. This is the wedding feast to come. There is also the kingdom now, the church living in exile in the world, awaiting Christ's return.

STUDIO WORK | *IDEA EXCHANGE*

1. How does anamnesis operate or thrive in our daily lives?

   Do we talk about God's purposes, or do we act and live them? Would this action cause us to stand out in the world?

2. How are an acorn and a book both examples of prolepsis?

   Do you see your daily actions as a part of God's plan for all things? Do you wake up knowing that each day has a purpose, that you have a purpose, for the life of the world?

3. How is anamnesis expressed in the Passover festival and in the communion table?

Does your church remember it is the lived memory of Christ in the world? What is the role of communion in your life, your church? Does it function as a deep and abiding reminder of our gift of life in Christ and our daily activities as his body in the world? Exodus 12:14 recounts the Passover: "This is a day you are to commemorate; for the generations to come you shall celebrate it as a festival to the Lord—a lasting ordinance." Luke 22:19 recalls communion: "This is my body given for you; do this in remembrance of me."

4. How is the consummation of God's kingdom "unfolding in the now"?

When someone becomes a Christian, and the Holy Spirit enters in, how does the "kingdom come" begin at that moment? God calls you with a purpose to work in his plan for all things. How does this calling change you as well as bless others? Are you compelled to change any attitudes or ideas about the role of the church in the world?

5. What does it mean to say "let it be" to God's plan and our part in his divine and wondrous mystery?

Are you active in seeking the welfare of the city, knowing God is always at work in the world through his church?

6. Jesus was beaten and bruised when he gave his life as an offering for the life of the world. How is the church called to serve in a broken world in need of God's healing?

Should we close the shutters and wait for the consummation of all things, or should we walk out our doors and actively seek ways to bless a hurting world?

7. How is the church like a family, and how are we to work together as the body of Christ in the world?

God's design for a family is to be *pointed out*, offering God-given gifts to the world. How might the church truly live as the family of God in the world?

PORCH STEPS | *HELLO WORLD*

1. What does it mean to be "scattered seed" in the world? How might you give yourself away, scattering the seeds of blessing in your life?

2. Knowing that your daily tasks have true purpose in the *not yet now*, does it affect how you approach your work? What would it mean to prepare the way of the Lord in your daily life? How does God's grace at work in this process transform you?

3. The *kingdom come* is already taking place in our priestly calling as Christ's body in the world. Does this change your view of the world and your place in it? Does the promise of the wedding feast, God's complete restoration of creation to himself, give you joy? Do you share this hope with others?

LANTERN LIGHT

Ezekiel 36:33–36 *They will say, 'This land that was laid waste has become like the garden of Eden; the cities that were lying in ruins, desolate and destroyed, are now fortified and inhabited.'*

Jeremiah 31:3–6 *I have loved you with an everlasting love; I have drawn you with unfailing kindness. I will build you up again …*

Isaiah 33:20 *Look on Zion, the city of our festivals; your eyes will see Jerusalem, a peaceful abode, a tent that will not be moved ...*

Colossians 1:17–20 *He is before all things, and in him all things hold together.*

Revelation 21:1–5 *I saw the Holy City, the new Jerusalem, coming down out of heaven from God, prepared as a bride beautifully dressed for her husband.*

PRAYER JOURNAL

1. Thank you, Father, that as your grace flows through the church to a fractured world, you transform us and prepare us for communion with you. Thank you that our lives and our work in the *not yet now* have a purpose in your plans for the renewal of creation.

2. Lord, give us the strength, wisdom, and humility to be your body in the world. Help us to be the hands and feet of Christ as we labor in exile and await your kingdom come. The earth belongs to you. We belong to you. You are the Gift-giver.

READ MORE

Ballor, Jordan J. *Get Your Hands Dirty: Essays on Christian Social Thought (and Action)*. Eugene, Ore.: Wipf & Stock, 2013, pp. 113–62.

Kuyper, Abraham. *Rooted & Grounded: The Church as Organism and Institution*. Translated and edited by Nelson D. Kloosterman. Grand Rapids: Christian's Library Press, 2013.